22.70

APR   2016

SPECTACULAR
SPACE SCIENCE

Exploring the
INNER
PLANETS

Nancy Dickmann

rosen publishing's
rosen
central®

New York

Published in 2016 by The Rosen Publishing Group, Inc.
29 East 21st Street
New York, NY 10010

Produced for Rosen by Calcium
Editors for Calcium: Sarah Eason and Jennifer Sanderson
Designer: Greg Tucker
Consultant: David Hawksett

Photo credits: Cover courtesy of NASA/JPL; p. 4 courtesy of Wikimedia Commons/NASA/Brian0918; pp. 4–5 © Dreamstime/Aaron Rutten; p 6. © Wikimedia Commons/ Tilemahos; p. 7 © Shutterstock/Oleg Golovnev; p. 8 courtesy of Wikimedia Commons/Loon, J. van (Johannes); p. 9 courtesy of Wikimedia Commons/Giovanni Schiaparelli; p. 10 courtesy of NASA; p. 11 courtesy of NASA/JHU APL/CIW; p. 12 courtesy of NASA; p. 13 courtesy of NASA/Nicolle Rager Fuller, National Science Foundation; pp. 14–15 © Dreamstime/Elephantopia; p.16 courtesy of ESA/P. Carril; p. 17 courtesy of ESA/Anneke Le Floc'h; p. 19 courtesy of Wikimedia Commons/NASA; pp. 20–21 courtesy of NASA/JPL; p. 22 courtesy of Wikimedia Commons/NASA; p. 23 © Dreamstime/Kenneth Sponsler; pp. 24–25 © Shutterstock/Andrew Barker; pp. 26–27 courtesy of NASA/JPL/Cornell; p. 27 courtesy of NASA/JPL; pp. 28–29 courtesy of NASA/JPL/Malin Space Science Systems; p. 29 top courtesy of NASA/JPL-Caltech; p. 29. bottom courtesy of NASA/JPL-Caltech/MSSS; p. 30 courtesy of Wikimedia Commons; p. 31 courtesy of NASA/JPL-Caltech/University of Arizona; p. 32 courtesy of NASA/JPL-Caltech/University Arizona/Texas A&M University; p. 33 courtesy of NASA; pp. 34–35 © Shutterstock/Pablo Hidalgo - Fotos593; p. 36 courtesy of NASA; p. 37 left courtesy of NASA; p. 37 right © Shutterstock/Algol; pp. 38–39; courtesy of Wikimedia Commons/Daein Ballard; p. 39 courtesy of NASA; p. 40 courtesy of NASA; p. 41 courtesy of JPL/NASA; p. 42 courtesy of Wikimedia Commons/Andrzej Mirecki; p. 43 courtesy of Wikimedia Commons/NASA; pp. 44–45 courtesy of Wikimedia Commons/NASA.

Library of Congress Cataloging-in-Publication Data

Dickmann, Nancy, author.
Exploring the inner planets/Nancy Dickmann.—First edition.
     pages cm.—(Spectacular space science)
Includes bibliographical references and index.
ISBN 978-1-4994-3629-7 (library bound)—ISBN 978-1-4994-3631-0 (pbk.)—
ISBN 978-1-4994-3632-7 (6-pack)
1. Inner planets--Juvenile literature. 2. Mercury (Planet)--Juvenile literature. 3. Venus (Planet)—Juvenile literature. 4. Mars (Planet)—Juvenile literature. 5. Outer space—Exploration—Juvenile literature. 6. Manned space flight—Juvenile literature. I. Title.
QB606.D53 2015
523.4—dc23

2014044944

Manufactured in the United States of America

CONTENTS

Chapter One
Welcome to the Solar System 4

Chapter Two
Mercury 10

Chapter Three
Venus 18

Chapter Four
Mars 26

Chapter Five
What Have We Learned? 34

Chapter Six
What's Next? 40

Glossary 46

For More Information 47

Index 48

WELCOME TO THE SOLAR SYSTEM

Somewhere within the vastness of the universe, hundreds of billions of stars swirl around a central point. It is not easy to find; this galaxy is just one of billions like it, strewn throughout the universe. On one of the galaxy's arms, about twenty-seven thousand light years from the center, lies a medium-sized star. The star is surrounded by rocky spheres, gaseous balls, icy lumps, and countless fragments of rock.

Out of the millions of objects that orbit the sun, eight of the largest are classified as planets.

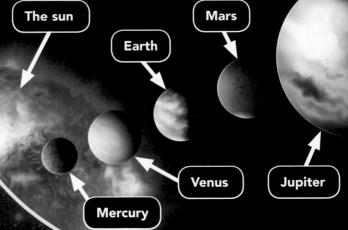

The sun

Earth

Mars

Venus

Jupiter

Mercury

That medium-sized star is the sun, and we live on one of those rocky spheres. The four planets closest to the sun—Mercury, Venus, Earth, and Mars—are relatively small and rocky. The other four—Jupiter, Saturn, Uranus, and Neptune—are much larger and mainly made of gas, with no solid surface.

This is what the size of the planets look like relative to each other.

Uranus

Neptune

Saturn

WHAT MAKES A PLANET?

In 2006, the definition of what a planet is changed. A planet must orbit the sun, and it must be large enough to have a nearly round shape. It must be gravitationally dominant in its orbit. This means that no other objects of a similar size orbit the sun in the same path. The small, rocky dwarf planet, Pluto, meets the first two requirements. It does not, however, meet the third, so it was demoted and is now considered a minor planet.

The inner planets may seem similar at first, but they have significant differences. Mercury is tiny and hot, with a heavily cratered surface. Venus is swathed in thick clouds that give it a stifling and toxic atmosphere. Earth has an atmosphere and is mostly covered with huge oceans of liquid water that are teeming with life. Mars has not one but two small, lumpy moons.

In this book we will explore the inner planets in detail, looking at what we know about them and how we learned it. Venus and Mars are some of the most-explored bodies in the solar system, and the missions that have traveled there have beamed back an impressive amount of data about our neighbors in space.

Early Beliefs

The inner planets can be easily seen with the naked eye, so they have been known since ancient times. Many cultures associated them with gods and goddesses. Even the earliest astronomers realized that planets were different from stars. The stars we see from Earth appear to rotate every twenty-four hours, but they do not change position relative to each other. The planets, on the other hand, move across the sky over a period of days, and that is how they get their name: *planetes* means "wanderers" in ancient Greek.

Mercury's pace is anything but wandering. It moves across the sky faster than any other planet, so both the Greeks and the Romans named it after their messenger god. Mercury, the Roman version, was famous for moving quickly between Earth and the heavens.

Many cultures, including the ancient Romans, have named the planet Venus after their goddess of love and beauty.

Like Mercury, Venus is between Earth and the sun, so it was known to several cultures as a morning star and an evening star, with separate names for each. The Babylonians realized these stars were the same planet more than 3,500 years ago. Venus is the closest planet to Earth, which is partly why it appears brighter than the other planets. Many ancient cultures viewed Venus as a female planet. One reason for this was that it was visible for about nine months a year, the same amount of time as a woman is pregnant.

Mars has a reddish color, even when seen with the naked eye, making it stand out from the other planets. As a result, most ancient cultures associated it with bloody war and death. The Sumerians named it after Nergal, their god of war, and the Greeks and Romans did the same: Ares for the Greeks and Mars for the Romans.

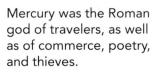

Mercury was the Roman god of travelers, as well as of commerce, poetry, and thieves.

ONE OR TWO?

The Mayans charted the motion of the planet Mercury. Records of their detailed observations include the appearance of Mercury as a morning star in 733 BCE and as an evening star in 727 BCE. The Mayans also calculated that Mercury would rise and set in the same place in the sky every 2,200 days.

For centuries, scientists followed the Earth-centered view of the universe proposed by the Greek astronomer Ptolemy (c. 100–c. 170 CE).

History of Astronomy

Although early astronomers were able to track and predict the movement of the planets, there was a lot they did not know. For example, since the planets appear roughly the same size as stars, they did not realize that the stars are so much farther away. They also did not know how the solar system was organized. Many early astronomers put Earth at the center of the solar system (and, indeed, the whole universe).

MYSTERIOUS LADY

No matter how good their telescopes were, astronomers never used to be able to see anything on the surface of Venus. The planet is surrounded by thick clouds, completely blocking the view. The first sighting of Venus's surface was not until 1975, when a Russian probe landed there and sent back photographs.

One thing they did know was that Mercury and Venus were closer to Earth than the sun was. The two planets pass between Earth and the sun, and if the alignment is just right, they can be seen as small black circles traveling across the sun. This is called a transit. As a result of this, most early solar system diagrams had the moon orbiting closest to Earth, followed by Mercury, Venus, the sun, and then Mars and the rest of the planets.

Once telescopes were invented in the early 1600s, astronomy really took off. The Italian astronomer Galileo Galilei (1564–1642) made a major breakthrough when he discovered that Venus has phases. This means that it appears to change shape like the moon does, slowly growing from a crescent shape to a full disc, and then back again. The change in shape is not visible to the naked eye, so Galileo was the first to see the phases of Venus. Mercury also has phases, but Galileo's telescope was not powerful enough to let him see them.

Before long, telescopes were powerful enough to show detail on the surface of the planets. Giovanni Schiaparelli (1835–1910), an Italian astronomer, observed linear features on Mars. He called them *canali*, meaning "channels," but this was mistranslated as "canals." Canals are man-made, so this led to speculation that there was intelligent life on Mars.

Schiaparelli used his observations to draw detailed maps of the surface of Mars.

9

Chapter Two

MERCURY

Although Mercury is relatively close to Earth, its position near the sun makes it difficult to view from Earth and also difficult for spacecraft to visit. As a result, we know less about it than we know about planets such as Jupiter and Saturn, which are much farther away. In the 1880s, Schiaparelli used a telescope to map part of Mercury's surface, a project that was continued in the 1930s by the Greek astronomer, Eugenios Antoniadi (1870–1944).

In the 1960s, astronomers started using radar to learn about Mercury. Using radar involves sending microwave radiation toward an object such as a planet and analyzing the signals that bounce back. It is similar to the way a bat uses echolocation to find insects to eat, sending out sounds and listening to how they bounce back. The technique can provide information about the planet's shape and surface features.

The MESSENGER spacecraft has taken amazingly detailed photographs of Mercury's surface, including the image shown right.

Only two probes have visited Mercury so far. The first, Mariner 10, was launched in 1973 to study Venus and Mercury. After completing a flyby of Venus, it used Venus's gravitational force to bend its path toward Mercury. Mariner 10 was not able to enter orbit around the planet, but it conducted three flybys, looping around the sun between each one. On its third approach, the probe came within 203 miles (327 kilometers) of Mercury's surface, but ran out of fuel before it could loop around the sun again. It is still in orbit somewhere around the sun.

Much of what we know about Mercury comes from the MESSENGER mission that launched in 2004 and finally entered orbit around the planet in 2011. Its goal was to study the planet's composition, geology, and magnetic field. It was a huge success. It mapped Mercury's entire surface in detail, as well as making many other discoveries.

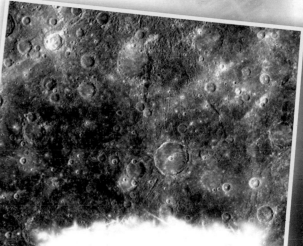

This image of Mercury's surface was taken by the MESSENGER spacecraft. The planet's cratered landscape can be clearly seen.

VISITING MERCURY

It is difficult to get a spacecraft into orbit around Mercury. For one thing, its nearness to the sun means that the sun's gravity is felt more strongly and disrupts a probe's orbit. Also, the changes in speed necessary to successfully enter orbit around the fast-moving planet would require a huge amount of rocket fuel.

Geology of Mercury

Photographs from Mariner 10 showed us that Mercury's surface looks a lot like the moon, covered with craters of various sizes as well as dark lava plains, mountains, and valleys. At one time in the distant past, Mercury was geologically active. This means that its surface was changing and shifting as a result of the effects of volcanoes and other geological processes. However, now there are no lava flows to cover over the impact craters left when other objects crash into its surface.

Mariner 10 mapped only about half of Mercury's surface, so it was not until the MESSENGER mission sent back data that we were able to see the rest of the planet in detail. These images showed that Mercury's surface is more jumbled than that of the moon. The largest crater, Caloris Basin, is about 960 miles (1,550 km) wide. The impact that created it was so huge that on the opposite side of the planet, it left an odd, hilly area, known as the "Weird Terrain."

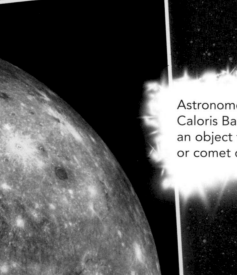

Astronomers believe that the Caloris Basin was formed when an object the size of an asteroid or comet crashed into Mercury.

GETTING SMALLER

Some of Mercury's more unusual features are the folds (called rupes) that run across the plains. Astronomers believed that these rupes were formed when the planet's interior cooled, making the whole planet shrink. The crust had already solidified and was now too big for what was inside, so it wrinkled as the planet shrank.

Mariner 10 discovered that Mercury had a magnetic field, which was one of the first clues about Mercury's core.

Mercury is equally weird on the inside. Like the other rocky planets, it has a metal core, surrounded by a thick, slowly moving mantle of hot rock, with a rocky crust on the outside. However, its core must be huge, making up nearly half of its volume. Astronomers can infer this based on data about the planet's density and size. One theory is that Mercury was once much bigger, but a large object crashed into it, blasting away much of the mantle and crust while leaving the core intact. Another idea is that the heat of the young sun vaporized much of its surface rock. One of MESSENGER's goals is to learn more about the core.

13

A Speedy Planet

Based on its movement across the sky, astronomers have known since ancient times that Mercury orbits the sun approximately once every eighty-eight days. As it is so close, the sun's gravity exerts a huge force on the tiny planet, making it travel quickly: about thirty miles per second (48 km per second)! Mercury's path is elliptical (a little like a squished circle), and when it is at its closest point to the sun, it travels more quickly.

It proved to be much more difficult to learn how fast Mercury rotated on its axis. Until the 1960s, many astronomers believed that Mercury was "tidally locked." This would mean that it took the same amount of time to rotate on its axis as it did to complete one orbit of the sun, causing the same side of the planet always to face the sun. Earth's moon is tidally locked in this way, which is why we always see the same side of it from Earth.

Mercury's rotation period was one of the first things discovered by using the Arecibo radio telescope in Puerto Rico. You may recognize it from the 1995 James Bond film *GoldenEye*!

However, radar astronomy in the 1960s showed that the dark side of Mercury was much hotter than would be expected. If it never faced the sun, that side should be incredibly cold, but this was not the case. From this data, scientists extrapolated a rotational period of about fifty-nine days. This was a surprise to the scientific community, and some tried to think of other ways to account for the high temperatures. In the end, data from Mariner 10 confirmed the shorter rotation. Giuseppe Colombo (1920–1984), an Italian astronomer, noted that for every two orbits of the sun, Mercury rotates three times on its axis.

VULCAN

In 1859, a French astronomer named Urbain Le Verrier (1811–1877) noticed anomalies in Mercury's orbit. He thought they were caused by the gravitational pull of another object orbiting closer to the sun. After all, Le Verrier had already used similar anomalies in Uranus's orbit to successfully predict the existence of Neptune. He named this hypothetical planet Vulcan, and for years, astronomers searched for it in the skies. Vulcan does not exist, but it was not until 1915 that Albert Einstein's theory of general relativity explained the irregularities in Mercury's orbit.

15

BepiColombo

Compared to the other inner planets, Mercury has been neglected by astronomers. Even the Hubble Space Telescope does not study Mercury—pointing its delicate optics at something so close to the sun could damage them permanently. However, all that is changing with BepiColombo. The mission, named after Giuseppe Colombo, is a joint project of the European Space Agency (ESA) and the Japanese Aerospace Exploration Agency (JAXA).

BepiColombo is actually two separate spacecraft: the Mercury Planet Orbiter (MPO), which is built by ESA, and JAXA's Mercury Magnetospheric Orbiter (MMO). The MPO is focused on researching the surface and internal composition of the planet, while the MMO studies the planet's magnetosphere. They will travel together until they reach Mercury and go their separate ways. The MPO will orbit closer to the planet than the MMO.

The mission has a lot to do; astronomers hope that it will solve a lot of unanswered questions about Mercury. MESSENGER has sent back a huge amount of data about Mercury, and BepiColombo is designed to complement that. It has more measuring equipment and will follow a different orbit pattern. The MPO will travel closer to the planet's surface and should be able to take better photographs.

This artist's impression shows BepiColombo in orbit around Mercury.

One question researchers want to answer is whether Mercury's core is liquid or solid and why it is so large. They hope the MMO will return evidence of why such a small planet has a magnetic field, when even the larger Mars and Venus do not. The MPO will search for sulfur or water ice at the poles. Many of these discoveries will teach us more about the formation of the solar system.

Prior to launch, the MPO is placed in a test chamber so that it can be heated to remove any potential contamination.

WHAT MIGHT HAVE BEEN

The original plan for the BepiColombo mission included a small lander, the Mercury Surface Element. It would have been the first probe ever to land on the planet's surface, and was scheduled to operate for about a week. It would have carried cameras as well as tools for exploring Mercury's chemical composition and magnetic field, as well as a tiny rover. Unfortunately, this part of the mission was canceled in 2003 for budget reasons.

Chapter Three

VENUS

Venus is sometimes called Earth's twin, as a result of its similar size and orbital distance from the sun. However, telescopes, probes, and landers have shown that it is actually completely different—the last place in the solar system you would want to visit! In contrast to the beautiful bright object we see in the sky, closer observation has shown that Venus is a dangerous, inhospitable place.

In 1761, a Russian astronomer, Mikhail Lomonosov (1711–1765), discovered evidence that Venus had an atmosphere. Venus has thick clouds, so it eluded close observation for centuries until astronomers started using other methods (such as radar mapping) in the 1950s and 1960s. In 1960, the Soviet spacecraft Venera 1 was launched. It was the first probe launched to another planet. However, it malfunctioned, and the National Aeronautics and Space Administration's (NASA's) Mariner 2 was the first to successfully fly past Venus, in 1962. It was followed by Mariner 5 and Mariner 10, which took photographs of Venus's clouds before traveling on to Mercury.

The Venera 3 probe crash-landed on Venus in 1966. It was the first spacecraft to reach the surface of another planet. In all, ten Soviet probes managed to land on Venus's surface, but the probes only managed to communicate with Earth for less than two hours. The high temperature and pressure on Venus destroyed probes within hours of landing.

More data has been retrieved by spacecraft entering into orbit around Venus. Venera 9 was the first spacecraft to enter orbit around Venus, in 1975. In addition to studying Venus's clouds and magnetosphere, it sent down a successful lander. Since then, several other probes have orbited Venus. In 1990, the NASA probe Magellan began its orbit around the planet. ESA's Venus Express mission entered orbit around Venus in 2006 and has sent back a huge amount of data. One key discovery is evidence that Venus may have had oceans in the past.

FINDING A WAY

Over the course of its four-year mission, Magellan was able to use radar mapping to "see" through the clouds on Venus. It provided incredibly accurate maps of 98 percent of the planet's surface.

USA

The Magellan spacecraft was carried into space on the space shuttle Atlantis.

Surface and Geology

Despite the number of spacecraft that have visited Venus, there is still a lot we do not know about the planet. For example, scientists do not have enough data to be confident about Venus's internal structure. Venus's size and mass are so close to that of Earth that we assume it has a core, mantle, and crust, like Earth does. We do know that since it was formed, Venus has been cooling at a similar rate to Earth, so its core is probably at least partially liquid, like Earth's is.

Thanks to the radar images provided by the Magellan spacecraft, we do know a lot about the surface. Most of it was shaped by volcanic activity, and measurements of sulfur in the atmosphere have led to theories that there might still be volcanic activity taking place on Venus. Some of the volcanoes on Venus are huge compared to those on Earth; there are more than 150 volcanoes that are more than sixty miles (97 km) across.

The highest volcano on Venus, Maat Mons, rises about three miles (4.8 km) from the planet's surface.

Most of the planet's surface is covered by smooth volcanic plains. There are also two large masses of higher land, which are often called continents. Unlike continents on Earth, these are not surrounded by oceans, but in the distant past, they might have been. Ishtar Terra, in the north, is about the size of Australia. Aphrodite Terra, in the south, is bigger.

Venus has fewer craters than Mercury, and they have not been eroded by wind or other impacts. None of them are smaller than two miles (3.2 km) across, because smaller objects would burn up while passing through Venus's thick atmosphere. Astronomers believe that volcanic activity has decreased dramatically since the last time the planet's surface was completely re-covered by lava.

RECYCLED PLANET?

There is no evidence of moving tectonic plates on Venus, so that means that its crust is not constantly "recycled" like Earth's is. Scientists estimate that Venus's crust is much older: about 300 to 600 million years old, as opposed to Earth's, which is 100 million years old.

An Inhospitable Place

In the time between the discovery of Venus's atmosphere in 1761 and the first radar mapping of its surface in the 1960s, many people believed that its clouds hid a lush planet, similar to Earth, with jungles or oceans covering the surface. However, modern observation techniques have shown us that Venus's atmosphere is anything but lush.

In the late 1950s, microwave observations showed extremely high temperatures on Venus: over 600 degrees Fahrenheit (316 degrees Celsius). No jungle or ocean could exist on a planet that hot! The thick, dense clouds, made up mainly of carbon dioxide, provide a vision of a greenhouse effect gone out of control. The clouds on Venus let in energy from the sun, then trap it there, with the result that Venus is the hottest planet in the solar system. It is hotter than Mercury, even though it is farther from the sun.

This image of Venus's swirling clouds was taken by the Pioneer Venus Orbiter in 1979.

WHAT'S IN THE AIR?

Twice every one hundred years or so, Venus transits the sun. The last pair of transits were in 2004 and 2012, and they were used by astronomers as an opportunity to study Venus's atmosphere. They were able to use spectroscopy to analyze sunlight passing through the planet's atmosphere and determine what chemicals it contained.

Venus appears as a black disc as it transits the sun.

Other readings showed lower temperatures, and scientists were not sure if the high temperatures existed on the planet's surface or up in its atmosphere. It turns out that high in the atmosphere, the temperature is lower, a little more like Earth's. One interesting theory is the possibility that life—in the form of tiny microbes—may exist there. Long ago, when Venus still had oceans, they may have contained life. When the thick atmosphere caused the planet to heat up and the oceans to evaporate, these life forms could have adapted to live in the clouds. More research is needed to prove or disprove this theory.

In addition to high temperatures, Venus has extremely high atmospheric pressure: about ninety times that of Earth. These two factors make manned missions to the planet's surface impossible. Even landers do not survive for long there before being crushed by the atmosphere.

23

Orbit and Rotation

Venus's path around the sun is nearly a perfect circle, and it completes one orbit about every 225 days. However, finding its rotation time proved to be very difficult. Astronomers had used the surface features on Mercury (such as craters) as landmarks to estimate how long it took to rotate. However, the clouds on Venus made that approach impossible. For example, the astronomer Jean-Dominique Cassini (1625–1712) lived before it was known that Venus had an atmosphere. He thought patterns in the clouds were surface features, and he estimated the rotation period as twenty-four hours.

This theory persisted for hundreds of years, and it was not until 1961 that radar was used to accurately measure Venus's rotation period at 243 days. That is longer than a year on Venus, and it is much longer than anyone had thought. What was even more unusual was the discovery in 1964 that Venus's rotation is retrograde.

Most planets rotate in the same direction as they orbit the sun. If you could look down at the solar system from above, you would see the planets moving counter-clockwise around the sun at the same time as they rotate counter-clockwise on their axes. However, although Venus travels counter-clockwise around the sun like the rest of the planets, it rotates clockwise on its axis.

There is still a lot to learn about Venus. Solar Probe+ will fly past Venus in 2018 on its way to the sun, and BepiColombo will conduct flybys in 2019 and 2020, although its main target is Mercury. Other missions have been planned and are awaiting approval, including one that would take samples of the surface and study the composition of the crust in more detail.

The telescope at Jodrell Bank Observatory in England played a key role in discovering Venus's rotation period.

A DAY ON VENUS

The combination of Venus's long days, relatively short years, and retrograde rotation make for an unusual calendar. If you could stand on the surface of Venus, you would see the sun rise in the west and set in the east. It would take almost 117 days from sunrise to sunset, though!

25

Chapter Four

MARS

Without a doubt, after Earth, Mars is the best-explored planet in the solar system. Dozens of spacecraft have been launched to study the planet, and as a result, we know a huge amount about it. The first spacecraft to reach Mars showed that many of astronomers' previous ideas—including theories about oceans, plants, and life on the planet—were wrong.

After a number of failed attempts, NASA's Mariner 4 probe flew past the planet in 1965, taking the first close-up photographs of the surface of another planet. The information it sent back about Mars's surface, temperature, and atmospheric pressure led to a rethink of designs for landers. A Soviet lander mission was launched in 1971, and although its orbiter was successful, the lander crash-landed. A second lander, later in the same year, became the first to successfully land on the planet. The Viking 1 and Viking 2 probes, launched in 1975, were a huge success, and their landers sent back crucial information about the planet's weather and magnetosphere.

Robot rovers have taken some amazing photographs of Mars's surface, such as this one from the Opportunity rover.

I CAME ALL THIS WAY...

The Soviet Mars 3 mission was the first lander to achieve a soft landing on another planet (as opposed to just crashing into the surface). The probe had taken more than six months to reach the planet, but it transmitted for only 14.5 seconds before the signal failed. It sent back just one partial photograph.

The Mars Global Surveyor spacecraft took just under two hours to complete an orbit of Mars. It did this over and over as it mapped the surface.

The year 1997 marked the beginning of the age of the rover, when the Mars Pathfinder mission landed the wheeled robot Sojourner. It was followed in 2003 by the Mars Exploration Rover mission, which put Spirit and Opportunity on the surface of the planet. The much larger Curiosity rover landed in 2012.

While rovers moved across the surface of Mars, a series of orbiters continued to study the planet from the skies. The Mars Global Surveyor mission carried out detailed mapping from 1999 to 2001, followed by the Mars Odyssey and Mars Express missions. The MAVEN orbiter and the Mangalyaan orbiter reached Mars in 2014 to study the planet's atmosphere.

Driving Around

Aside from the moon, Mars is the only body in the solar system to have been explored by robotic rovers. These small wheeled vehicles can send back information that would be impossible to obtain from an orbiting spacecraft. For example, rovers can dig into rocks and carry out detailed chemical analysis. The way they move over the surface gives us more information about what it is like.

We now know that the surface of Mars is dry, dusty, and rocky. The surface is covered by a thin layer of iron oxide (commonly called rust), which gives it its red color. Giant sandstorms sometimes sweep across the planet, blocking the view of the orbiters circling it. Mars's surface does not have moving tectonic plates like Earth does, so this has led to the formation of large volcanoes (now inactive) and also the deepest valley in the solar system. The tallest mountain in the solar system, Olympus Mons, is on Mars.

It is likely that at one point, the surface was very different, with liquid water covering the planet in rivers and oceans. Now, the temperature and atmospheric pressure are both too low to allow liquid water to exist on the planet's surface. However, there is ice there, which is easily visible in the form of an ice cap at its north pole.

Early landers returned photographs showing what looked like dry riverbeds and canyons. More recent missions have sent back data confirming the presence of ice beneath the surface of the planet. In 2014, the Curiosity rover discovered that the soil where it is exploring contains about 2 percent water ice. This could be a huge help to any astronauts who visit Mars in the future, since carrying water with them from Earth is not very practical.

This artist's impression shows the Curiosity rover on the surface of Mars.

Curiosity took this selfie of its sample processing tool. It can put powdered rock into the small hole to be analyzed.

A LASTING IMPRESSION

Impact craters are common on Mars, because its extremely thin atmosphere offers it very little protection. Craters on Mars can last a long time, because there is no liquid water and little wind to erode them, and there are no active volcanoes to cover them with lava.

29

Movement and Moons

In the seventeenth century, the German astronomer Johannes Kepler (1571–1630) studied the movement of Mars. At that point most people assumed that the planets followed perfectly circular paths around the sun (or around Earth, as some still believed). However, Mars's movement did not match up. Kepler used math to figure out that the planet must follow an elliptical path, with the sun not quite at the center. When Mars was closer to the sun, it traveled a little faster. Other planets also orbit like this, and the discovery helped Kepler formulate his laws of planetary motion.

Mars rotates around its axis once every twenty-four hours, thirty-nine minutes, and thirty-five seconds, making the length of a day on Mars almost identical to a day on Earth. However, the Martian year is nearly twice as long at 687 Earth days. Mars's axis also tilts at a similar angle to Earth, giving it seasons. However, because of Mars's irregular path, the seasons are not all the same length. For example, spring lasts for seven months, and winter for just four. Even in the summer, it is not hot: it might reach 65 degrees Fahrenheit (18 degrees C) during the day and drop to -130 degrees Fahrenheit (-90 degrees C) at night.

Johannes Kepler began his career as an assistant to the Danish astronomer Tycho Brahe (1546–1601) before carving out his own place in history.

THIS PLACE HAS NO ATMOSPHERE

The Martian atmosphere is so thin that it is hardly there at all: it is about 1 percent of Earth's atmosphere. It is mainly made up of carbon dioxide, but it is too thin to trap the sun's heat and cause a greenhouse effect. As a result, temperatures can drop to -225 degrees Fahrenheit (-143 degrees C) at the poles during winter.

Phobos is being pulled steadily toward Mars. Eventually, it will be torn apart by Mars's gravity.

Unlike Mercury and Venus, Mars is not alone in its patch of the solar system. It is orbited by two small moons, Deimos and Phobos. Compared to Earth's moon, they really are tiny: Deimos is fewer than eight miles (13 km) across, and Phobos is about fourteen miles (22.5 km) in diameter. They are lumpy and irregularly shaped, and they orbit very close to the planet. In 1971, when Mariner 9 visited Mars and found it covered by a dust storm, it studied and photographed Phobos while waiting for the dust on Mars to clear.

Life on Mars?

Ever since Giovanni Schiaparelli's drawing of "canals" on Mars, people have been fascinated by the idea that life exists there. Although we know that the Martians of science-fiction books and movies do not exist, the possibility remains that simple life in some form existed on Mars in the past and may still exist today. After all, there was once abundant liquid water on the planet, and there is still ice. Any life on Mars would have to be different from most life on Earth. For example, there is no oxygen in the Martian atmosphere, and the temperature is extremely low.

The Viking landers in the 1970s carried out simple tests to see if there were microbes in the soil. They took a sample of soil and exposed it to chemicals that would feed any microbial life living there. Some gases were produced, which could have been the result of microbes' life processes. However, most scientists now think the results can be explained by chemical processes.

The Phoenix lander was the first mission to return data from either of Mars's polar regions.

The Phoenix lander explored Mars in 2008 with the goal of finding a zone within the planet's soil where microbial life could exist. The lander could not drive around, but it had a robotic arm that allowed it to dig trenches. It discovered that Mars's soil contains a toxic chemical called perchlorate, which is harmful to life. Several years later, the Curiosity rover found even more perchlorate.

However, Curiosity also found several positive signs. It explored the remains of a former freshwater lake and found chemicals that form naturally in drinkable water, where life could form. It has also detected key elements such as carbon, hydrogen, nitrogen, and phosphorus. In 2014, its mission was changed to focus on the search for organic molecules—the building blocks of life.

This meteorite from Mars, nicknamed "Black Beauty," was discovered in 2011 in the Sahara Desert.

MARTIANS INVADE EARTH!

No Mars mission has ever brought back soil samples to Earth, but scientists have found at least thirty-four meteorites that we know came from Mars. Three of these show possible evidence of ancient life: tiny structures resembling fossilized bacteria. There is no definitive proof either way, but scientists continue to analyze these amazing rocks.

33

Chapter Five

WHAT HAVE WE LEARNED?

The invention of the telescope in the early 1600s revolutionized astronomy, leading to amazing new discoveries about the solar system. However, since the Space Age began in the late 1950s, our knowledge about the planets themselves has increased at an even greater rate. In addition to sending astronauts to the moon, unmanned probes have mapped the craters of Mercury, peered through the clouds of Venus, and rolled across the rocky surface of Mars.

Some people question why we spend so much time, effort, and money studying other planets. After all, they say, there are serious problems—such as climate change and disease—on Earth. Should we not focus on solving our own problems before worrying about the ancient history of Venus?

Dr. John Spencer, a scientist who worked on the Cassini mission that studied Saturn, once said, "Well, you know, you can spend your life in your house, or you can get out and get to know your neighborhood." This is what NASA, ESA, and other space agencies are doing. By studying Earth's near neighbors in space, we are gaining important insights into how Earth and the rest of the solar system formed.

We cannot discover how planets form and change by studying only Earth. The world we know is the result of complex forces that have operated for billions of years. Things might have worked out very differently if Earth was closer to the sun, had a thinner atmosphere, or had an axis tilted at a different angle. Studying other planets also gives us insight into the future. For example, conditions on Venus and Mars offer clues as to what Earth might be like in billions of years.

Despite what people believed in the past, we now know that Earth is the only place in the solar system to contain lush plant and animal life.

A CROWDED FIELD

At the beginning of the Space Age, the United States and USSR went head-to-head, each trying to outdo the other and be the first to reach key milestones. Since then, other countries have played their part. ESA joined the field in the mid-1970s, and in recent years Japan, China, and India have become major players. The Indian Space Research Organisation (ISRO) sent a mission that entered Mars's orbit in 2014, succeeding on its first attempt.

Could We Live There?

One question that space exploration has tried to answer is whether humans could live on other planets, either permanently or temporarily. After all, astronauts live on the International Space Station (ISS) for months at a time. One day, it may become necessary for humans to colonize other worlds in order to survive. Another reason for setting up colonies on other worlds would be to make use of their resources, by mining valuable substances and sending them back to Earth.

Living on another planet would mean recreating conditions similar to Earth. Human colonists would need air to breathe, water to drink, and food to eat. They would need to be protected from extreme temperatures and solar radiation. They would also need to find a way of remaining fit and healthy in places with lower gravity and atmospheric pressure.

The ISS provides everything that astronauts need to live, though supplies must all be sent up from Earth.

FLOATING CITIES?

It would be virtually impossible to set up a colony on the surface of Venus, where the temperature is hot enough to melt lead. About thirty miles (48 km) above the surface, however, the atmosphere provides a potential habitat. The atmospheric pressure and temperature are similar to Earth's, and scientists have proposed floating cities held up by balloons.

These illustrations show what a colony on Mars might look like.

Mercury's position near the sun would make colonization difficult; any settlement would have to be near the poles. However, Mercury does have a magnetic field, which could help protect colonists from cosmic rays and solar storms. Its gravity is less than Earth's but still about twice that of the moon. Mars is the most likely candidate, but it would still be incredibly difficult. It has water, but it is very cold and has no atmosphere or magnetosphere to protect colonists from radiation.

The first step toward setting up a colony would be to send a manned mission to explore the planet and then return. However, even that presents significant challenges. For example, a trip to Mars would take at least six months, and with current technology it would be impossibly expensive to send the huge amount of water, food, and other supplies astronauts would need.

37

Terraforming

Some scientists have taken the idea of colonization a step farther and explored the possibility of "terraforming" other planets. This literally means "Earth-shaping," and it involves deliberately changing a body to be more like Earth. The idea may sound like science fiction, and that is one of the origins of the concept. However, we have already seen that human actions play a role in the weather and other conditions on Earth. Is it really such a huge leap to think that we could change conditions on other planets, too?

Mars is one of the main candidates for terraforming. Its thin atmosphere is mainly carbon dioxide, which is a greenhouse gas, so if we could thicken the atmosphere it would help heat the planet. Heating the planet would release more carbon dioxide, currently frozen at the poles, and accelerate the heating process. However, Mars's lack of a magnetic field like Earth's is a significant problem, and at the moment, the technology to provide a planetary-scale magnetic field does not exist.

Terraforming Mars would be a long, slow process, but the planet might eventually end up with liquid oceans once more.

Terraforming Venus would require reducing the surface temperature and changing the atmosphere by getting rid of most of the carbon dioxide and sulfur dioxide and replacing it with nitrogen and oxygen. Venus receives about twice as much sunlight as Earth, so one possible way of reducing the temperature would be to put up a large solar shade. Another idea is to introduce bacteria into the atmosphere, which would take carbon from the atmosphere.

REVERSE TERRAFORMING

In his 1898 novel The War of the Worlds, the author H.G. Wells (1866–1946) tells the story of a Martian invasion of Earth. The Martians bring a type of red weed from Mars, which grows so quickly that it engulfs the native Earth plants. This is a kind of reverse terraforming, in which Earth is transformed to be more suitable for alien species.

At the moment, terraforming is just a concept. Scientists have not yet developed all the technologies that would be needed, and no missions are planned. In addition, many people question the ethics of terraforming and wonder if humans have the right to alter other planets.

The astronomer Carl Sagan (1934–1996) proposed terraforming Venus by introducing algae into the atmosphere in order to remove some of its carbon dioxide.

Chapter Six

WHAT'S NEXT?

No matter how much we discover about other planets, there is always more to learn. Space missions take years to plan and prepare, so while one probe is in orbit around a distant planet, the next two or three are already in the pipeline. For example, Venus is scheduled to be visited in the near future by BepiColombo (on its way to Mercury) and Solar Probe+ (on its way to study the sun). Missions farther into the future, such as Russia's Venera-D, designed to map future landing sites, are already in the planning stages. Engineers are working on a way to design a lander that can last for more than a few hours in Venus's harsh conditions.

At the moment, though, most attention is focused on Mars. There are multiple rovers and landers on the surface, with several probes in orbit around the planet, and there are many more planned. One proposed mission will set up a network of meteorological stations to provide a clearer picture of the planet's weather. Still another will try to return a sample of Martian soil to Earth.

"Robonaut" was designed to work alongside astronauts, and it can use tools in the same way a human can.

One proposed mission to Mars will include a lander equipped with a drill and other tools for studying the planet's internal structure.

The missions that get all the headlines, though, are manned missions to Mars. Several space agencies have proposed sending astronauts to Mars before 2040. Some plans involve sending colonists on a one-way trip. However, there are many technological hurdles to clear before such a mission could succeed.

DO WE NEED ASTRONAUTS?

Humans are not really designed for long space flights. We need a lot of food and water, we produce waste that has to be disposed of, and we have a habit of getting sick or injured. Some people have proposed sending robots instead of humans to Mars. After all, a robot does not need to be fed, and it will not get bored during the years of travel. There is already a robot working on the ISS. Could the next step be to send a robotic astronaut to Mars?

41

The Future of Space Exploration

Future missions to other planets face significant challenges. For one thing, the distances involved are huge. It takes most spacecraft between six and twelve months to reach Mars. That is fine for a robot but difficult for a living, breathing human. Using more fuel could make the trip go faster, but that would mean taking a huge load of fuel, which brings us to the second problem: weight. Launching anything into space is expensive; currently it costs about $10,000 for every pound you want to launch into space. A rocket capable of carrying several people to Mars will not be light!

Space engineers are having to think outside the box to come up with ways to solve these problems. New technologies may allow spacecraft to go faster and farther and to do it more cheaply. One innovation, the ion drive, has already been put to the test and is in use on the Dawn probe, which is studying asteroids. Another idea, using a solar sail, requires no fuel at all. Instead, it relies on the force of the "solar wind"—the pressure of radiation from the sun.

Solar sail technology has been successfully tested on the JAXA spacecraft IKAROS.

Scientists are hard at work on other technologies to enable astronauts to travel to other planets. In addition to new methods of powering spacecraft, engineers must develop more efficient ways of recycling water and air and providing food, as well as methods of protecting them from the high levels of radiation they will encounter.

HOW DOES AN ION DRIVE WORK?

An ion drive works by bombarding a gas (usually xenon) with electrons. This turns the atoms of gas into positively charged ions, which move around at high speeds. When the ions reach a high enough speed, they are focused into an ion beam that shoots out the back and thrusts the spacecraft forward. The amount of fuel needed is small compared to a conventional rocket engine, and ion drives can achieve much higher speeds.

In this test of an ion drive, you can see the charged atoms coming out of the engine.

43

Could It Be You?

NASA sent twelve astronauts to the surface of the moon in the 1960s and '70s, but since then, no human has traveled more than a few hundred miles above Earth's surface. Space travel is both expensive and dangerous, and once astronauts reached the moon, the focus shifted to unmanned probes. We have learned a great amount from the spacecraft that have visited other planets, but can it compare to the thrill of seeing an astronaut broadcast live from the surface of Mars?

Until recently, it was only the governments of large countries that were able to launch space missions. However, in the past decade, more private companies are getting involved. Some hope to make money by taking tourists into space, while others are focused on goals such as sending astronauts to Mars. Part of this is driven by economics. NASA, for example, is allowing private companies to take over the delivery of cargo and crew to the ISS. More competition could mean better prices.

Several lucrative prizes have sparked interest in space flight and led to huge investment in new technologies. The Ansari X Prize, announced in 1996, offered $10 million to the first commercial organization to launch a reusable manned spacecraft into space twice within two weeks. The Google Lunar XPrize, launched in 2007, offers a $30 million prize for privately funded missions to land a robot on the moon.

Whether it is a government agency or a private company that sends the first astronaut to another planet, it will take a huge team to get them there. Research into all aspects of space technology is needed, and some of those technologies may prove useful on Earth as well. Who knows—maybe you will be the person who designs them!

SPACEX

One of the top private companies in spaceflight research is SpaceX. The company has developed the reusable Falcon launch vehicles, as well as the Dragon spacecraft, which will eventually carry astronauts to the ISS. In 2012, it became the first private company to send a spacecraft to the ISS.

The original version of the Dragon spacecraft can carry only cargo, but SpaceX is working on a new version that will be able to transport astronauts.

45

GLOSSARY

astronomers Scientists who study planets, stars, and other objects beyond Earth.

atmosphere The layer of gases surrounding a planet.

atmospheric pressure The pushing force of the weight of the gases in the atmosphere.

axis An imaginary line through the center of a planet, around which it rotates.

craters Hollow areas, like the inside of a bowl, created when an object crashes into a planet or other large object.

flyby A flight past an object to make observations. When a spacecraft does a flyby of a planet, it does not stop or enter orbit.

galaxy Hundreds of billions of stars and other matter held together by gravity.

gravity The force that pulls all objects toward each other.

lander A spacecraft designed to land on the surface of a planet or other object and send back data.

light years Units of distance equal to the distance light can travel in one year–about six trillion miles (9.46 trillion km).

magnetic field The space around a magnet in which a magnetic force is active.

magnetosphere The region surrounding a planet or other object in which its magnetic field is the dominant magnetic field.

meteorites Lumps of stone or metal from meteors that have landed on Earth.

microbes Tiny living things that can be seen only with a microscope. Bacteria are a type of microbe.

microwave A type of high-frequency radio wave. It can be used to send information over long distances.

orbit The curved path that one body in space takes around another, such as a moon orbiting a planet.

poles The ends of a planet's axis.

probe An instrument or tool used to explore something that cannot be observed directly.

radar The use of radio waves to track the location, distance, and speed of faraway objects. Waves are sent out and then picked up again when they bounce back after hitting an object.

radiation Waves of energy sent out by sources of heat or light, such as the sun. Radiation can be harmful to living things.

retrograde Moving in the opposite direction. Venus has a retrograde rotation on its axis: clockwise as opposed to the other planets' counter-clockwise.

rover A robotic vehicle that is capable of driving across the surface of a planet, moon, or other object in space.

solar system The sun and everything in orbit around it, such as planets, asteroids, and comets.

tectonic plates The segments of Earth's crust that move around in relation to one another. Movement of tectonic plates causes earthquakes and volcanoes.

terraforming Causing changes to another object in space that will make it more like Earth.

transit When a planet or other object passes directly between Earth and the sun, so that it can be seen from Earth as it moves across the disc of the sun.

FOR MORE INFORMATION

Books

Aguilar, David A. *Space Encyclopedia: A Tour of Our Solar System and Beyond.* Washington, D.C.: National Geographic Kids, 2013.

Maxwell, Scott, with Catherine Chambers. *Mars Rover Driver* (The Coolest Jobs on the Planet). Chicago, IL: Heinemann-Raintree, 2014.

Oxlade, Chris. *Mars* (Astronaut Travel Guides). Chicago, IL: Heinemann-Raintree, 2013.

Rusch, Elizabeth. *The Mighty Mars Rovers: The Incredible Adventures of Spirit and Opportunity* (Scientists in the Field). Boston, MA: HMH Books for Young Readers, 2012.

Thomas, Isabel. *Mercury and Venus* (Astronaut Travel Guides). Chicago, IL: Heinemann-Raintree, 2013.

Websites

Due to the changing nature of Internet links, Rosen Publishing has developed an online list of websites related to the subject of this book. This site is updated regularly. Please use this link to access the list:

http://www.rosenlinks.com/SSS/Inner

INDEX

Antoniadi, Eugenios 10
atmospheric pressure 23, 26, 28, 36

BepiColombo 16–17, 24, 40

Caloris Basin 12
Cassini, Jean Dominique 24
Cassini mission 34
Colombo, Guiseppe 14
craters 5, 11, 12, 21, 24, 29, 34
Curiosity 27, 28, 29, 33

Deimos 31

Earth 4, 5, 6, 7, 8, 9, 10, 14, 18, 20, 21, 22, 23, 26, 28, 30, 31, 32, 33, 34, 35, 36, 37, 38, 39, 40, 44
European Space Agency (ESA) 16, 18, 34, 35

Galilei, Galileo 9
gas 4, 32, 38, 43
gravity 11, 14, 31, 36, 37
greenhouse effect 22, 31, 38

Indian Space Research Organisation (ISRO) 35
International Space Station (ISS) 36, 41, 44, 45
ion drive 42, 43
Ishtar Terra 21

Japanese Aerospace Exploration Agency (JAXA) 16, 42
Jupiter 4, 10

Kepler, Johannes 30

lava 12, 21, 29
Le Verrier, Urbain 15
Lomonosov, Mikhail 18

Magellan 18, 19, 20
magnetic field 11, 13, 17, 37, 38
magnetosphere 16, 18, 26, 37
Mariner probes 11, 12, 13, 14, 18, 26, 31
Mars 4, 5, 7, 9, 17, 26–33, 34, 35, 37, 38, 39, 40, 41, 42, 44
Mars Exploration Rover 27
Mars Global Surveyor 27
Mars Pathfinder 27
MAVEN 27
Mercury 4, 5, 6, 7, 9, 10–18, 21, 22, 24, 31, 34, 37, 40
MESSENGER 10, 11, 12, 13, 16
microbes 23, 32
moons 5, 9, 12, 14, 28, 30–31, 34, 37, 44

National Aeronautics and Space Administration (NASA) 18, 26, 34, 44
Neptune 4, 15

Olympus Mons 28
Opportunity 26, 27
orbit 4, 5, 9, 11, 14, 15, 16, 18, 24, 27, 30, 31, 35, 40

Phobos 31

radar 10, 14, 18, 19, 22, 24
retrograde rotation 24, 25
rupes 13

Saturn 4, 10, 34
Schiaparelli, Giovanni 9, 10, 32
Sojourner 27
Solar Probe+ 24, 40
solar system 4–9, 17, 18, 22, 24, 26, 28, 31, 34, 35
Spencer, Dr. John 34
Spirit 27
sun 4, 5, 7, 9, 10, 11, 13, 14, 15, 16, 18, 22, 23, 24, 25, 30, 31, 34, 37, 40, 42

tectonic plates 21, 28
telescopes 8, 9, 10, 14, 16, 18, 25, 34
terraforming 38–39
transit 9, 23

universe 4, 8
Uranus 4, 15

Venera probes 18, 40
Venus 4, 5, 6, 7, 8, 9, 11, 17, 18–25, 31, 34, 36, 39, 40
Venus Express 18
Viking probes 26, 32
volcanoes 12, 20, 28, 29
Vulcan 15

water 5, 17, 28, 29, 32, 33, 36, 37, 41, 43